AMAZING MIGRATIONS

ON THE MOVE WITH GREAT WHITE SHARKS

by Rebecca Donnelly
illustrated by Alan Brown

GRASSHOPPER

Tools for Parents & Teachers

Grasshopper Books enhance imagination and introduce the earliest readers to fiction with fun storylines and illustrations. The easy-to-read text supports early reading experiences with repetitive sentence patterns and sight words.

Before Reading

- Discuss the cover illustration. What do readers see?
- Look at the glossary together. Discuss the words.

Read the Book

- Read the book to the child, or have him or her read independently.
- "Walk" through the book and look at the illustrations. Who is the main character? What is happening in the story?

After Reading

- Prompt the child to think more. Ask: What is the White Shark Café? Why do great white sharks gather there?

Grasshopper Books are published by Jump!
5357 Penn Avenue South
Minneapolis, MN 55419
www.jumplibrary.com

Library of Congress Cataloging-in-Publication Data

Names: Donnelly, Rebecca, author.
Brown, Alan, illustrator.
Title: On the move with great white sharks
Rebecca Donnelly; illustrated by Alan Brown.
Description: Minneapolis, MN: Jump!, Inc., [2023]
Series: Amazing migrations | Includes index.
Audience: Ages 7-10
Identifiers: LCCN 2021060802 (print)
LCCN 2021060803 (ebook)
ISBN 9781636908854 (hardcover)
ISBN 9781636908861 (paperback)
ISBN 9781636908878 (ebook)
Subjects: LCSH: White Shark–Migration–
Juvenile literature.
Migratory animals–Juvenile literature.
Classification: LCC QL638.95.L3 D659 2023 (print)
LCC QL638.95.L3 (ebook)
DDC 597.3/3-dc23/eng/20220110
LC record available at https://lccn.loc.gov/2021060802
LC ebook record available at https://lccn.loc.gov/2021060803

Editor: Eliza Leahy
Direction and Layout: Anna Peterson
Illustrator: Alan Brown

Printed in the United States of America at
Corporate Graphics in North Mankato, Minnesota.

Table of Contents

Across the Ocean

Hello! I'm Greta. I'm a great white shark. I have more than 300 sharp teeth!

I'm looking for seals and sea lions to eat. I'm fast. I can swim 35 miles (56 kilometers) per hour!

I come close to shore during the fall mating season. I mate near Guadalupe Island, Mexico.

After mating, I head to the open ocean. Great whites spend most of our time alone. I won't see my mate again. I try to stay away from male sharks when I'm pregnant. They can be dangerous!

mate

I'm not like most fish. I don't lay eggs. My pups grow inside me for a year and a half. They grow slowly because the ocean is so cold. That's why my migration takes two years! At the end of it, I'll give birth to my pups.

It's winter now. I swim to warmer waters. That will help my pups grow.

This part of the ocean is called the White Shark Café. It's an enormous area between Mexico and Hawaii.

Many male sharks come here during winter to find food. Their migration only lasts one year. I'll stay for a while, but then I'll move on.

This is Greg. I'm not getting too close to him, but watch him dive! Males here dive more than 100 times a day. They can go 1,400 feet (427 meters) down. There aren't seals here to eat, but there is plenty of other food.

Greg eats tiny fish, squid, and phytoplankton. They move with the sunlight. They rise at night and fall during the day. Greg chases them by bobbing up and down.

Female sharks don't bob. We dive and stay deep underwater during the day.

I keep swimming. I’ll spend another year in the open ocean. I go as far as Hawaii!

Spring and summer is pupping season. It's time for me to give birth. I swim to the coast of Baja, California.

pups

My pups can swim as soon as they're born. We won't stay together. They will find their own food and take care of themselves.

I don't want to run into any male sharks for a while, so I'm swimming away again to the open ocean. I'll be back in fall for mating season!

Range Map

Great white sharks are born near the coast, but they travel in the open ocean as they get older. Scientists are still learning about their migration patterns. Take a look at where they live!

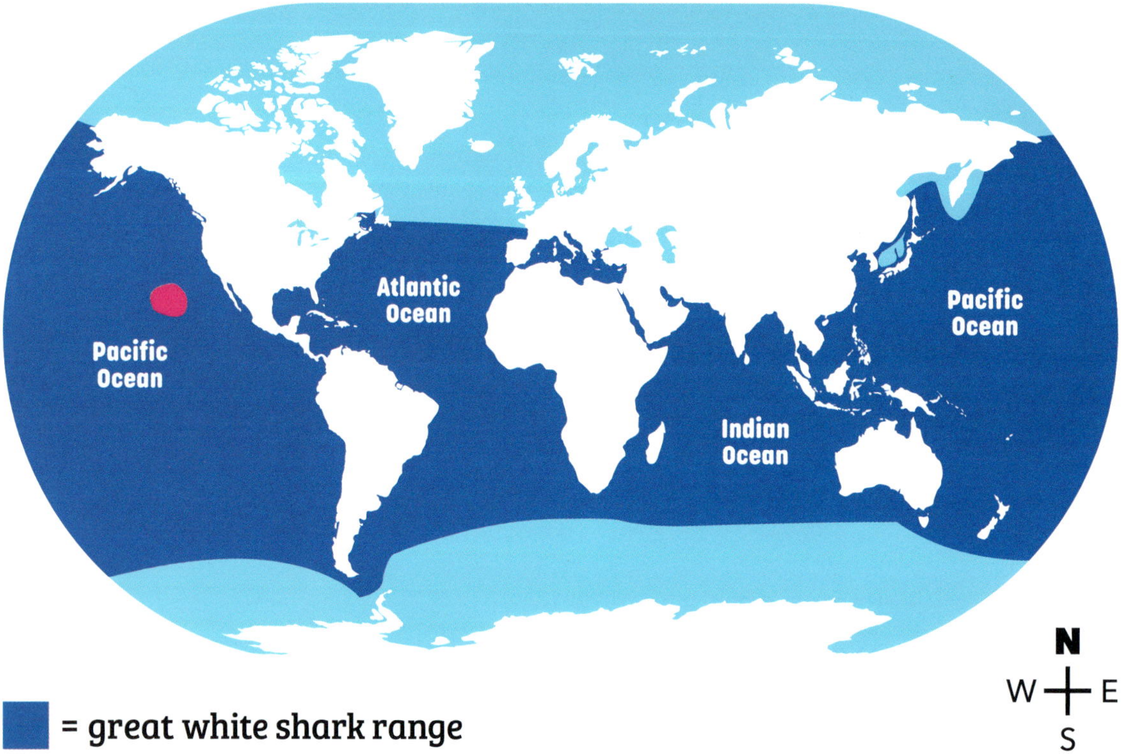

= great white shark range

= White Shark Café

Let's Review!

Why does Greta's migration take two years?

A. She is a slow swimmer.

B. She migrates farther than any other animal.

C. Her pups grow inside her for 18 months.

Glossary

bobbing: Moving up and down in a short, quick manner.

mate: To join together to produce young.

mating season: The time of year, usually fall, when sharks mate.

migration: The movement of animals from one area to another.

phytoplankton: Tiny plants that live in the ocean.

pregnant: Having a baby or young developing inside the body.

pupping season: The time of year, usually spring and summer, when shark pups are born.

pups: Baby sharks.

White Shark Café: An area of the Pacific Ocean between Mexico and Hawaii where great white sharks gather in winter.

Let's Review! Answer Key: **C.** Her pups grow inside her for 18 months.

Index

To Learn More

FACT SURFER

Finding more information is as easy as 1, 2, 3.

1. Go to www.factsurfer.com
2. Enter "**onthemovewithgreatwhitesharks**" into the search box.
3. Choose your book to see a list of websites.